People Around Town / Gente de mi ciudad

MEET THE BAKER/
TE PRESENTO A LOS PANADEROS

By Joyce Jeffries   Traducción al español: Eduardo Alamán

Gareth Stevens
Publishing

Please visit our website, www.garethstevens.com. For a free color catalog of all our high-quality books, call toll free 1-800-542-2595 or fax 1-877-542-2596.

Library of Congress Cataloging-in-Publication Data

Jeffries, Joyce.
 [Meet the baker. English & Spanish]
 Meet the baker = Te presento a los panaderos / Joyce Jeffries.
     p. cm. — (People around town = Gente de mi ciudad)
 ISBN 978-1-4339-7382-6 (library binding)
 1. Baking—Juvenile literature. 2. Bakers—Juvenile literature. I. Title. II. Title: Te presento a los panaderos.
 TX683.J4418 2013
 664'.752092—dc23
                               2011049254

First Edition

Published in 2013 by
Gareth Stevens Publishing
111 East 14th Street, Suite 349
New York, NY 10003

Copyright © 2013 Gareth Stevens Publishing

Editor: Katie Kawa
Designer: Andrea Davison-Bartolotta
Spanish Translation: Eduardo Alamán

Photo credits: Cover Echo/Cultura/Getty Images; p. 1 JupiterImages/Brand X Pictures/Thinkstock; pp. 5 Otna Ydur/Shutterstock.com; p. 7 Guy Shapira/Shutterstock.com; p. 9 Morgan Lane Photography/Shutterstock.com; p. 11 JupiterImages/Photos.com/Thinkstock; p. 13 Grauvision/Shutterstock.com; pp. 15, 24 (batter) Mike Neale/Shutterstock.com; pp. 17, 24 (oven) iStockphoto/Thinkstock; p. 19 JupiterImages/Goodshoot/Thinkstock; p. 21 erwinova/Shutterstock.com; pp. 23, 24 (apron) Jack Hollingsworth/Digital Vision/Thinkstock.

All rights reserved. No part of this book may be reproduced in any form without permission in writing from the publisher, except by a reviewer.

Printed in the United States of America

CPSIA compliance information: Batch #CS12GS: For further information contact Gareth Stevens, New York, New York at 1-800-542-2595.

Contents

A Baker's Job 4

Making a Cake 10

A Baker's Tools 18

Words to Know 24

Index. 24

- -

Contenido

El trabajo de panadero 4

Haciendo un pastel .10

Los utensilios 18

Palabras que debes saber 24

Índice 24

A baker makes bread.
He makes cookies
and pies too.

Un panadero hace pan.
También hace galletas
y pastelillos.

5

Some bakers make cakes!

¡Algunos panaderos hacen pasteles!

7

A baker works at a bakery. He works early in the morning.

El panadero trabaja en la panadería. El panadero trabaja muy temprano.

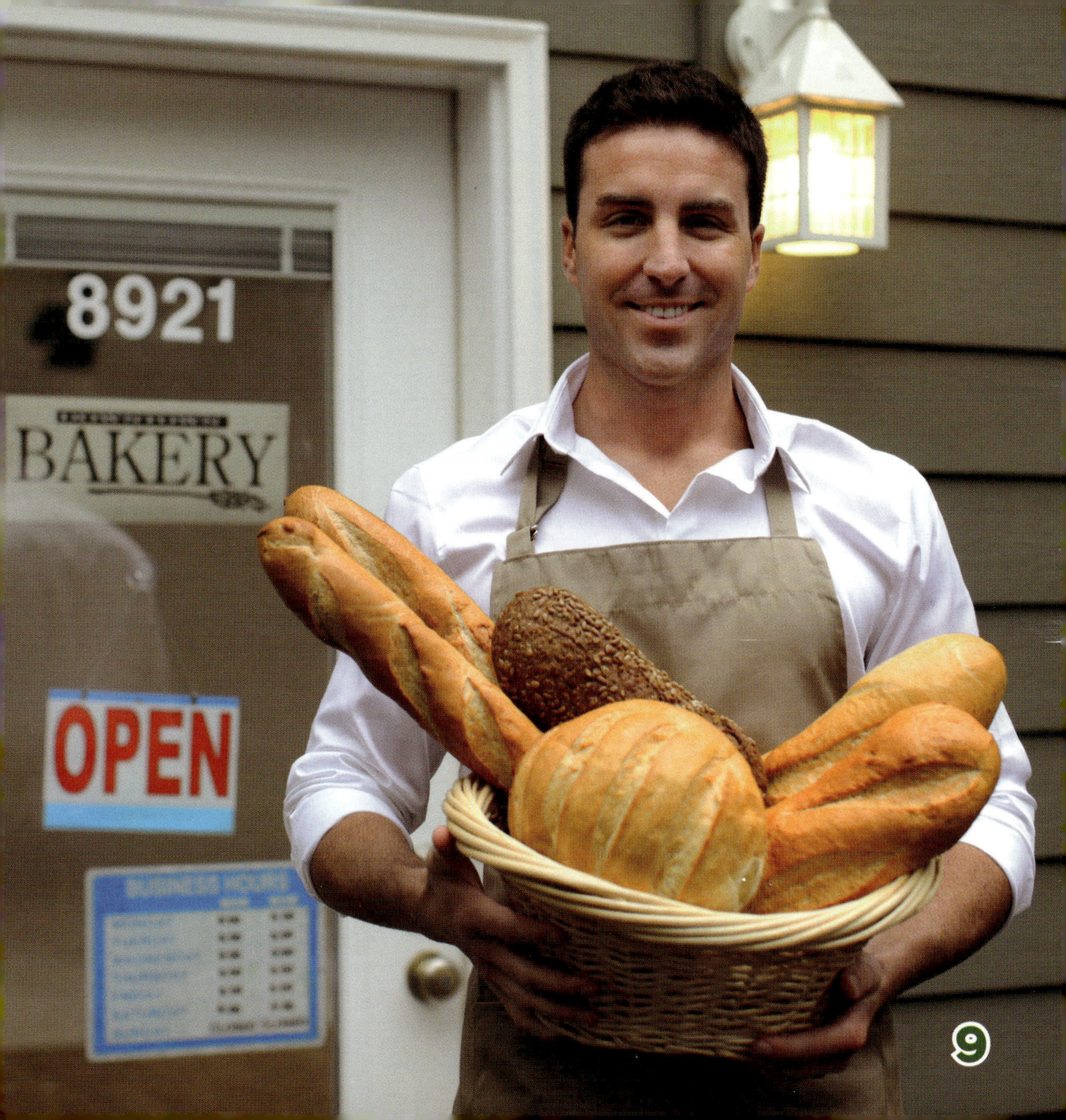
8921
BAKERY
OPEN

Bakers mix things
in a bowl.

Los panaderos mezclan
sus ingredientes
en un bol.

11

They mix eggs, water, and flour. This makes batter.

Los ingredientes pueden ser huevos, agua y harina. Esto forma la masa.

13

Batter is used
to make a cake.

Esta masa se usa para
hacer pasteles.

15

It goes in an oven.
The oven is very hot!

La masa se pone en el horno. ¡El horno está muy caliente!

17

Bakers use many tools.

Los panaderos usan muchos utensilios.

19

One tool is a knife.
This cuts bread.

Uno de sus utensilios es el cuchillo. El cuchillo corta el pan.

21

A baker wears an apron. It keeps her clothes clean.

La panadera usa un delantal. El delantal mantiene su ropa limpia.

23

Words to Know/
Palabras que debes saber

apron/
(el) delantal

batter/
(la) masa

oven/
(el) horno

Index / Índice

bread/(el) pan 4, 20

cakes/(los) pasteles 6, 14

cookies/(las) galletas 4

pies/(los) pastelillos 4

Friends of the
Houston Public Library

664.752 J HACRX
Jeffries, Joyce.
Meet the baker =Te presento a los
panaderos /
ACRES HOMES
11/12